Steamers of the Clyde

Queen Alexandra racing the Duchess of Argyll, 1935.

Twenty five years ago John Nicholson and the late George Stromier collaborated in publishing in Scottish Field a selection of illustrated histories of their favourite Clyde steamers. Their delightful words and paintings were later collected into book form – a collectors' item – which has long since been out of print. The present authors have the good fortune of joining with John Nicholson in publishing this second edition.

The motor ships which appeared in the first edition have been omitted and Duchess of Argyll, Saint Columba and Waverley have been added. Many of John Nicholson's original paintings have been replaced with even better artwork. These paintings allow us to appreciate and savour the colours of those steamers which were scrapped before colour photography became popular.

Mr. Stromier's text has only been altered to correct obvious errors and where updating was required, amended to preserve accuracy. The text for the three new steamers has been written by Ian Maclagan.

This book is not a complete history of the Clyde steamer; it is, to quote from the foreword to the first edition, a record of some of the vessels which formed part of the finest fleet of pleasure steamers in the world. We hope the reader will enjoy these "Memories of the Clyde".

Tom Hart
Ian Maclagan
David G. Will

STEAMERS of the CLYDE

by GEORGE STROMIER and JOHN NICHOLSON

A 'SCOTTISH FIELD' PUBLICATION IN FULL COLOUR 10s 6d

A reminder of 'Steamers of the Clyde' as produced by 'Scottish Field' in 1967.

Contents

R.M.S. "COLUMBA"   J. NICHOLSON.

P.S. Columba

By 1877, David MacBrayne, who had been junior partner in the shipping firm of David Hutcheson and Company, had become virtually the controller; two years later it bore his name.

From the extreme north of the West Highland seaboard down to Loch Fyne Hutcheson boats held the monopoly, so it was something of a shock in that year to find a new enterprise, the Glasgow and Inveraray Steamboat Company, placing a magnificent new vessel called **Lord of the Isles** on the Inveraray station. Not only were they invading taboo territory but their steamer out-classed every other boat on the Firth - and that included Hutcheson's pride and joy, the **Iona**.One year in the role of second fiddle was more than enough for MacBrayne, who thereupon placed an order with J. and G.Thomson of Clydebank for a ship which would eclipse this latest "swan of the Clyde". The outcome was **Columba.**

Majestic was the only description suitable for her. She was MacBrayne's showpiece and attained a prestige never before or since reached by any of the river craft. Her fame was world-wide and in the latter months of the Victorian and Edwardian summers the cream of society would board her as a stepping stone on the Royal Route to their shoots and lodges in the Highlands.

Columba's hull, with its curved bow in the pattern of her older "sister" **Iona**, was beautifully modelled and her great oscillating engines ran with great smoothness, driving her through the sea with a placid motion. Her speed placed her among the fleetest of the Clyde greyhounds and her length of over 300 feet has not been equalled in the Clyde passenger fleet. Among her additional appointments were a post office and a barber's shop and in the former department the mail was stamped, stored and delivered at the various calling points at a rate of over 100,000 letters a month.

Such then was the magnificent vessel which took up the Tarbert and Ardrishaig sailing in 1878 and maintained it for 58 summers with scarcely a break in routine.

Columba's voyaging was confined to the holiday months and it was rare for her season to extend into even the first week of October. By that time she was snugly tucked away in Bowling Harbour (Greenock in her latter years) and did not emerge until the following May had run its course. During the Clyde coasting seasons disturbed by the 1914-18 war **Columba** remained in home waters, but did her sailing out of Wemyss Bay, the Cloch-Dunoon boom having curtailed her normal route. She returned to her Glasgow berth when peace was restored.

To the dismay of her countless admirers she appeared for the 1929 season with her glossy black hull painted grey. So great was the outcry against this affront that within the month she was back to her accustomed garb.

At the close of the 1935 summer she retired with the **Iona** to Greenock Harbour for the last time. When they emerged it was but to make the short trip, under tow, to the shipbreaker's yard at Dalmuir.

G.S.

P.S. Ivanhoe

Passengers who imbibed well rather than wisely became something of a problem on the Clyde river steamers in the 19th century, so much so that in the 1870's a consortium of businessmen decided to run a vessel on strictly teetotal lines. They formed the Firth of Clyde Steam Packet Company and on February 25, 1880, a 225-foot long paddle steamer was launched at the yard of D. and W. Henderson. She was given the name **Ivanhoe** and although she made her headquarters at Helensburgh she was not connected with the North British fleet then based there. After the launch the guests were entertained by the builders in the model-room at Meadowside, when a rather incongruous note was struck by the speeches being toasted in wine!

Ivanhoe was a twin funnel saloon steamer, typical of the period, with narrow alleyways running down the outside of the main and fore saloons. The normal refreshment bars, however, were conspicuous by their absence. On May 3 she underwent her trials and at the beginning of June went into service. On her opening cruise she encountered both **Glen Rosa** and **Sheila** on the route to Arran when, sad to relate, the new ship came off worst.

Her daily run was by way of Greenock Custom House Quay, Princes Pier, Kirn, Dunoon, Wemyss Bay, Rothesay, Tighnabruaich, Corrie and Brodick to Lamlash. On Mondays, Wednesdays, and Fridays she extended her voyage to King's Cross and Whiting Bay. During her first season a special extra run was made on Saturdays either to Campbeltown, round Arran or round Ailsa Craig. Later on Pladda was the objective of the extra sail which then gave way to an evening cruise, a form of excursion which this steamer inaugurated and popularised.

Another new steamer, **Scotia,** had to deputise for **Ivanhoe** in the first week of her service as **Ivanhoe** broke down after leaving Wemyss Bay and had to be towed into Rothesay by the steam yacht **Matador.** Her first two seasons, however, were so successful that in September, 1881, the local press carried a report that four Clyde yards had been asked to estimate for building three more steamers to expand the Firth of Clyde Company's business.

Under the command of Captain James Williamson, who was also part owner, **Ivanhoe** continued to prosper (although she did not get any additional fleet units to assist her). Captain Williamson left her at the close of the decade to become Marine Superintendent of the new Caledonian Steam Packet Company.

In the spring of 1894 **Ivanhoe** went south for the opening of the Manchester Ship Canal but was back in her native waters for the start of the summer season. Three years later she was bought outright by the C.S.P. Company - although to all intents and purposes she had been plying under their supervision for some time - and bars were installed.

Her new owners placed her on ordinary coast connections from the railway termini and she was no longer regarded as a cruise boat. The year 1911 found her again changing hands, this time on the Broomielaw run for a firm known as the Firth of Clyde Steam Packet Company. They changed her yellow funnels to white and later added narrow black tops. By 1914 she was in the hands of Turbine Steamers Limited, who lengthened the black funnel tops to the conventional depth. She was running frequently to Lochgoilhead at this time but when the war curtailed the sailings she was chartered to the Caledonian company and once again became a railway boat. At first she ran from Rothesay to Wemyss Bay but later was engaged solely above the Dunoon-Cloch boom on the Gourock, Kirn, Dunoon station.

In 1920 **Ivanhoe** was handed back to Turbine Steamers but lay in harbour at Greenock until she made the sad passage to the breaker's yard at Dumbarton.

G.S.

P.S. Grenadier

The MacBrayne fleet down the years has included some really handsome vessels, but there was surely no finer looking craft to carry the famous red and black funnel than **Grenadier**, launched in March, 1885, from the Clydebank yard of J. and G. Thomson.

This statement must be qualified to exclude the first 16 years of **Grenadier's** existence. Originally she possessed two rather spindly looking funnels which detracted from the balanced beauty of her hull design but, after she was reboilered in 1902, the sight of her graceful form gliding over the Firth of Clyde or West Highland waters was sufficient to gladden the heart of any artist.

Grenadier, 222 feet in length, had full-width saloons both fore and aft, brightened by the insertion of large observation windows. Under her little bow and bowsprit she carried the carved figure of a grenadier. A pair of oscillating engines gave her a speed of a little over 16 knots.

Although **Grenadier** put in many weeks of service in her 42 years she was, strictly speaking, hardly a Clyde pleasure steamer. Much of her time was spent outwith the Clyde estuary with Oban as her base and it was only in the off season that she put in an appearance on MacBrayne's Ardrishaig run.

Having completed her trial trip through the Kyles of Bute to Glen Sannox, Arran and back to Princes Pier, **Grenadier's** first service was to Loch Fyne until **Columba** relieved her early in June, 1885. Then she made her way round the Mull of Kintyre to Crinan and ran from there to Oban and Fort William. At the height of the season she was transferred to the Oban, Loch Scavaig, Loch Coruisk, Portree and Gairloch run. Later she took over the Staffa and Iona cruise and was identified with this route almost continuously throughout her career.

There was a break in continuity after reboilering in the winter of 1902/3. The ensuing summer saw her on the Clyde with her headquarters at Rothesay, where she left each morning at 8.15 for the Broomielaw, retracing her path each afternoon at 1.30. On Saturdays she extended her route to Tighnabruaich and circled the Island of Bute.

As one would expect of a vessel designed for open water work, **Grenadier** proved a useful unit in the Royal Navy's minesweeping service during the 1914-18 war. Her naval service was without incident and she returned to Irvine in March, 1919, for reconditioning and was soon back on her summer service to Iona.

Grenadier's peace-time activities were in contrast to her carefree naval career. In January, 1902, she damaged her stern in a collision with a dock wall. Five years later her figurehead had to be replaced after she had collided with another vessel, and in November of the same year she ran aground and was holed off Gourock during a dense fog on the Firth.

Further trouble was avoided until January, 1925, when, though in fine fettle after overhaul (she was clipping 25 minutes off her normal time between Rothesay and Ardrishaig), she broke a shaft. She was back on duty, however, within a fortnight. But disaster fell on the night of September 6, 1927, while she lay at the North Pier, Oban. Fire broke out and spread so rapidly that three of her crew failed to escape. One of the victims was her master, Captain Archibald McArthur.

After being made seaworthy and the paddlewheels removed, **Grenadier** was towed to Greenock, but a fuller inspection confirmed that the damage was beyond practical repair. The hull was towed to Ardrossan for dismantling and thus passed from active service the bonniest paddleboat to fly the MacBrayne colours.

G.S.

P.S. "MADGE WILDFIRE"   J. NICHOLSON.

P.S. Madge Wildfire

Although she started her career as **Madge Wildfire** and carried this title for the first 27 years of her life, this little paddle steamer is probably better remembered as the **Isle of Skye**.

The "Madge" entered the ranks of the Clyde river steamer fleet in 1886 as one of Captain Campbell's Holy Loch boats. She was a product of McKnight's yard in Ayr. At this time the Campbells had two vessels on the route, **Meg Merrilies** and **Waverley**, but the latter was too large and too fast for this service and was transferred to the Ayr route when **Madge Wildfire** made her appearance.

Ideally suited for the daily run to Kilmun from the Broomielaw, doing a steady 16 knots in the process, there was nothing particularly outstanding about the "Madge". She had only one saloon, a plainly furnished affair which extended from midships to near the stern.

After only three seasons with her original owners she changed hands. The Caledonian Steam Packet Company had just come into being and for a start they purchased the goodwill, stock and business of the Campbell concern. **Madge Wildfire** then changed her all - white funnel for the all - yellow one of the latest Clyde shipowners. She was kept on her usual route for a number of years and later served the Holy Loch from Gourock. Her new master evidently found her a more than useful boat as they kept her for the best part of a quarter of a century, during which period she deputised on occasion on the Millport or Rothesay runs. They also fitted her with a small foresaloon and, in 1903, transferred the bridge forward of the funnel and redesigned her paddleboxes from the fan shaped style to the horizontal slotted pattern.

In 1911 she again changed hands. A Captain Cameron of Dumbarton decide to go in for steamboat owning and his first acquisition was **Madge Wildfire**. In his service she made an assortment of cruises to the coastal resorts. It was apparently a paying proposition, for in the next year she was joined by another unit, the erstwhile North British steamer **Lady Rowena**. **Madge Wildfire's** sojourn with Cameron was of only two years' duration yet she managed to change the colour of her funnel twice. In her first year she had merely added a black top to her yellow "lum", but the next season the yellow was replaced by red. In this condition the hull was repainted in an unusual hue for the Clyde fleet—bottle green.

The 1913 change was to Buchanan. This fleet was short of a vessel after the departure of **Isle of Bute** for service in Morecambe Bay, so **Madge Wildfire** was bought in as a replacement and renamed **Isle of Skye**, with her funnel in the Buchanan colours of black with white band. She made her first run under the Buchanan flag on the 10.30 a.m. service from the Broomielaw to Dunoon, Rothesay and the Kyles of Bute. Thereafter she was placed on the 11 o'clock run.

In the first two years of the war she was still running from the Broomielaw, often to Millport before the anti-submarine boom was laid and then into the Gareloch, but by 1916 her name had disappeared from the Clyde fleet. The Admiralty had called her up as a fleet auxiliary and she saw service as a tender in the Cromarty Firth and as a minesweeper in the Pentland Firth.

After three years of strenuous naval work the little paddlesteamer came back to a much changed Clyde scene in March, 1919. The Williamson and Buchanan interests had merged to form a new company and **Isle of Skye** was the first vessel to sail for them.

Once again her funnel colouring had undergone a change. The Navy had painted her grey all over and her 1919 ensemble was white and black topped funnel, black hull and paddleboxes. Mostly she was on the Rothesay service with spells on the Millport run.

Early in 1927 Williamson-Buchanan sold her to the Grangemouth and Forth Towing Company Limited. Based at Leith, and with her name changed to **Fair Maid,** she made daily trips from Leith West Pier to Aberdour, Kirkcaldy and under the Forth Bridge to Kincardine and Alloa. The funnel, of course, was again repainted; this time to black top and buff base.

When war came again in 1939 **Fair Maid** was beyond active service but, garbed once again in grey, she was transformed into a decontamination vessel. The end of hostilities also saw the end of the little ship; she was broken up at Troon.

In one respect **Fair Maid**, ex Isle of Skye, ex Madge Wildfire, was surely unique among Clyde steamers; she sported no fewer than nine successive colour schemes on her well proportioned funnel.

G.S.

P.S. Lucy Ashton

Dandie Dinmont, one of the original ships of the North British when they began their Clyde service in 1866, was, after 22 years, deemed obsolete. To replace her, an order was given to Thomas Seath and Company of Rutherglen, and in May, 1888, **Lucy Ashton,** successfully negotiating the weir, went down river for completion and joined the other Sir Walter Scott "characters", **Jeanie Deans, Guy Mannering, Diana Vernon** and the little **Gareloch,** to give her services to Dunoon, the Holy Loch and occasional trips to Rothesay.

There was nothing outstanding in either the design or machinery of the new ship, although she certainly possessed a beautifully modelled hull. She had a comfortable, but not lavish, saloon aft, a miniature and rather austere one forward, a haystack boiler and a single diagonal engine capable of driving her at something under 17 knots. All in all, a handy little craft but definitely playing second fiddle to the two greyhounds already established in the fleet.

Later additions at Craigendorn relegated her to the Gareloch run but, if this was a more sheltered route that escaped the winter gales of the open Firth, there were other hazards just as threatening. The Gareloch was seldom free of laid up liners and, while these could be easily avoided during the hours of sunshine, they were a deadly menace in fog or bad weather.

Thus it was in December, 1910, during a severe snowstorm, that the Allan liner Siberian dragged her anchor and lay full in the track usually traversed by **Lucy Ashton**. The little Craigendoran paddleboat ran full tilt into the merchantman and had her bows stove in. Although badly crippled she got back to headquarters. Had she not been a worthy example of Clyde shipbuilding art a worse fate might have befallen her.

For close on 40 years **Lucy Ashton** did the selfsame run plus the ferry service over to Princes Pier. She escaped the call to the colours in both world wars and remained at home, a useful prop in the depleted Clyde passenger steamer ranks.

The Second World War saw her embark on the most strenuous period of her career. Although in her fifties, she was the sole unit of the Craigendoran fleet and carried on year after year with scarcely a pause in service. Necessary overhauls were usually performed on Sundays as she lay at her base.

Before the lifting of the anti-submarine boom her run did not extend beyond Dunoon, but when this was raised in 1945 she reopened the Craigendoran-Rothesay sailings and kept up this duty until the return of **Talisman** and **Jeanie Deans** from war service.

With the nationalisation of the railways in 1948 **Lucy Ashton** lost the funnel colouring of red, white and black with which the Craigendoran boats were associated... albeit during the war years her "lum" had been painted grey . . . and donned the less distinguished livery of buff and black. Towards the close of her career the old ship had risen in eminence from the position of one of the lesser lights of a once mighty fleet. She had won for herself an affection from war-weary Clydeside that surpassed that of any other vessel previously connected with the Clyde passenger trade. The Clyde River Steamer Club honoured her diamond jubilee with a special charter when, for a brief afternoon, she revisited many of her old haunts.

But in 1949 the writing was on the wall and she was towed to Faslane for breaking up. Souvenir hunters abounded and her siren was purchased by a Glasgow firm and given to a business in Santiago, Chile, where its high pitched tone still calls the workers to duty.

The Lucy's hull was retrieved from the breaker's yard and used for a brief spell by the British Shipbuilders Research Association in experimental tests connected with jet propulsion.

With the departure of **Lucy Ashton**, the Clyde passenger service severed its last link with the Victorian era.

G.S.

P.S. Duchess of Hamilton

The year after their debut on the Firth of Clyde the Caledonian Steam Packet Company added three new ships to their fleet, one of which was a very notable vessel, **Duchess of Hamilton**.

Built and engined by Denny at Dumbarton and launched in April, 1890, she was a lengthy boat of 250 feet. Her spaciousness was accentuated by the then novel design of having the promenade deck extended right forward to the bow and very nearly to the stern. The main saloon aft, furnished in the most luxurious Victorian style, was the full breadth of the vessel. Strangely enough, although the C.S.P.'s other new ships had foresaloons of similar width, **Duchess of Hamilton** had alleyways running down each side.

To Captain James Williamson, then Marine Superintendent of the Caley, she was the finest river steamer ever to grace the waters of the Clyde and he continued to laud her praises long after the arrival of newer tonnage. Despite his acclaim the "Duchess" was not as graceful as some of her sister "Duchesses", nor could she be included in the greyhound class for long. There was a noticeable absence of lift and sheer forward and, on her vast expanse of deck, the funnel and bridge were placed too close together to give a pleasing outline. But, for all that, she was a fine vessel. Designed as an 18-knotter she is recorded as having touched 18.1 knots on trial and is said to have held **Columba** in a trial of speed in her first year—no mean feat. She lost pace, however, fairly early in her career.

In the year of her launch, the Caledonian Railway had opened their route to Ardrossan in opposition to the Glasgow and South Western, and **Duchess of Hamilton** was intended to cater for the Arran trade. The Sou'West connection on this sea link was the Buchanan steamer **Scotia** and when the Caledonian representative appeared on the scene she had little difficulty in vanquishing her old-fashioned opponent. In two brief years, however, the opposition had secured the nucleus of a fleet of their own planning and, with the advent of **Neptune** and that quite remarkable craft **Glen Sannox**, it was the turn of the yellow funnel steamer to play second fiddle.

Nevertheless, **Duchess of Hamilton** remained a firm favourite on the Arran route and when she was transferred up river to Gourock in 1906 to make way for **Duchess of Argyll**, she carried her popularity with her. Here she was employed mostly on excursion work—round the Lochs, round Arran and Ailsa Craig or Ayr and Ailsa Craig-and was also a ready choice as club steamer at many of the Clyde regattas. In June, 1909, the Caley introduced the first Sunday rail connection to the coast and the "Duchess" performed this run. By 1911 she had changed her week-day schedule and was sailing daily to Arrochar.

The "Duchess" had one or two mishaps while serving on the Firth but they were all of a minor character. She was also in the news as a rescue ship, like the time in 1899 when she found **Jupiter** out of action with a stiff north-westerly gale blowing. **Duchess of Hamilton** was on her last run of the day from Ardrossan when she encountered **Jupiter** one and a half miles off the Arran coast. She stood by until tugs were summoned, then took off her rival's passengers and landed them on the mainland.

In the first World War she was commandeered as a naval auxiliary and, after some time on trooping duties, was fitted out for minesweeping. In this capacity, while in the company of the Thames pleasure steamer **Yarmouth Belle,** she was sunk on November 29, 1915, unfortunately with the loss of some of her crew, one of whom had served on her in peacetime on the Firth of Clyde.

G.S.

P.S. "LORD OF THE ISLES"   J. NICHOLSON.

P.S. Lord of the Isles

An Inveraray service via Dunoon, Rothesay and the Kyles of Bute was inaugurated in 1877 when a new company, the Glasgow and Inveraray Steamboat Company, placed a steamer which they named **Lord of the Isles** on this route. A highly successful vessel, she maintained this run for 13 summers before being bought by a London concern for service on the Thames.

To replace her for the 1891 season, the same builders, Messrs. D. and W. Henderson, Partick, were given the contract to construct a second and more up to date version, and so a second paddleboat bearing the title **Lord of the Isles** made her appearance on the Firth.

She was another extremely fine craft and a delight to the eye. Her widely spaced funnels of multicoloured design, backed by burnished copper steam pipes, helped to enhance her smart appearance. Unlike her predecessor, the saloons were built to the full width of the hull. Originally the foresaloon terminated just abaft the mast, but in 1895 the promenade deck was extended to the bow, giving her greatly increased carrying capacity. With a good turn of speed, the "Lord" maintained the high standard which her forerunner had established.

For the first dozen years of her existence she plied the Inveraray trade with great success, monarch of all she surveyed in Loch Fyne, but when the turbine **King Edward** appeared on the scene her monopoly ceased. Gradually the old paddle steamer's complements began to dwindle, and in 1912 Turbine Steamers Limited bought her and she was given a new route to travel. Starting at the Broomielaw daily at 10.30 she traversed the same course as far as Tighnabruaich, but then headed south to circumvent the Island of Bute before turning homeward.

Lord of the Isles was not requisitioned when war came in 1914 but sailed on from Glasgow to Lochgoilhead, as the anti-submarine defence boom barred her way southward beyond Dunoon. When the river was temporarily closed to cruising traffic she made her headquarters at Princes Pier.

After the armistice she resumed the "round Bute" run until the final year of her existence, 1928.

Having suffered a double blow in 1927 through the loss of both **Chevalier** and **Grenadier**, MacBrayne's fleet was under strength, so **Lord of the Isles** flew the famous West Highland pennant in her last year in service, on the Lochgoil and Arrochar route. At the end of the season she was condemned, and on October 24 was towed from Bowling Harbour to Port Glasgow for breaking up.

In a lifespan of 39 years, entirely free from mishap, she was served by only three captains, Donald Downie, Archie McAllister and Allan McDougall. The first mentioned had stepped from the bridge of the first "Lord" to his new command.

With her departure the Clyde not only lost a famous steamer, but another distinctive funnel colouring passed from the scene.

G.S.

P.S Glen Rosa

If for no other reason, **Glen Rosa** may be remembered as the last surviving member of the great Glasgow and South Western fleet. This company, which was later than the Caledonian and the North British in acquiring vessels to maintain its Clyde coast service, began operations with second-hand ships in 1891. The following year three new vessels were built and in 1893 two more were ordered, of which **Glen Rosa** was to be one. Shortly after construction began at Clydebank, the Belfast and County Down Railway took over one of the ships, naming her **Slieve Donard**. The two vessels were almost identical, but one had a more graceful sheer forward and aft. The Scottish railway claimed this boat and she took the name **Minerva**. A third craft identical to the Irish vessel, was then laid down and she became **Glen Rosa**.

Built to sturdy specifications, **Glen Rosa** and her near twin were intended for off season work on the Firth and to help out where required during the summer months. The promenade deck was not carried far beyond the mast, but the cutaway bow was covered over at bulwark level and railed off. The front end of the foresaloon was extensively strengthened and altogether a more formidable pair of winter boats could not be found anywhere. In the engine room the powerful little pair of diagonals were smaller editions of the heavy machinery characteristic of the Princes Pier boats and produced a good turn of speed. Towards the close of her career **Glen Rosa** had lost pace to a marked degree and those who were unfamiliar with her early success as a pacemaker were apt to hold her to ridicule.

She opened her career with a variety of cruises and when the summer had gone took up the winter run to Arran from Ardrossan. No Clyde steamer was better suited for this arduous task. **Glen Rosa** also appeared for a spell on the Loch Long route and took part in tendering work from Princes Pier.

During the First World War she acted as minesweeper, chiefly in the Belfast Lough and Irish Sea, when she bore the title **H.M.S. Glencross**. She was one of a group with **Kenilworth, Talisman, Caledonia, Marchioness of Bute, Marchioness of Breadalbane and Isle of Arran.** When the flotilla moved south to operate in the English Channel, **Glen Rosa** dropped out at Swansea to join another group.

On her return to the Clyde her summer season running was almost entirely devoted to the Millport and Kilchattan Bay route, at first from Fairlie and later from Wemyss Bay when she came under L.M.S. control.

Throughout her entire career only once do I know of her being in trouble. That was in March, 1930, when on the evening run from Ardrossan to Arran, a bracket in her port paddle snapped when on passage between Brodick and Lamlash. She was only a quarter of a mile offshore in Corriegills Bay and, as the sea was calm, she anchored. After her passengers had been landed by ship's boat, the Clyde Shipping Company's tug **Flying Swallow** towed her to Greenock.

Glen Rosa continued to serve Cumbrae until the final year of her existence when, as in her initial season, she was engaged in an assortment of cruises from the Clyde resorts.

Just before the declaration of war in 1939 she was taken to Arnott Young's at Dalmuir and broken up.

G.S.

P. S. "CULZEAN CASTLE"   J. NICHOLSON.

P.S. Culzean Castle

The season of 1895 found an " un-kent face " among the Clyde pleasure fleet, the paddle steamer **Culzean Castle**. Built at Southampton in 1891, she had been the property of the Bournemouth, Poole and Swanage Steam Packet Company, when she was known as **Windsor Castle**. A Scottish concern, the Glasgow, Ayrshire and Campbeltown Steamboat Company, judging her to be ideal for their service to Kintyre, purchased her and brought her north.

Culzean Castle was a big, beamy boat of 254 feet and was reputed to have touched 19 knots on her trials. She had a large single elliptical buff and black-topped funnel, two masts and saloons fore and aft, the former stretching just short of the foremast. Her bow was yacht-like in design but, strange to say, for a time she carried no bowsprit. In the forepeak there was an ample forecastle raised to the level of the promenade deck. Two other features of her design were novel on the Clyde. The saloons were lit by rounded ports instead of by conventional windows and in the engine room the machinery was a triple crank drive.

After a hurried overhaul she was put into service on the first day of June, 1895, under the command of Captain Alexander Gillies, late of Buchanan's steamer **Eagle**. Her run was from Princes Pier to Campbeltown, via Dunoon, Fairlie, Keppel, Lochranza, Pirnmill and Machrie Bay.

During her first season she suffered from machinery trouble; on one occasion an engine seizure on her way back from Campbeltown so delayed her that she berthed at Keppel in the region of 1 a.m. and still had to thread her way to her upper Firth base. Worst of all she suffered a further engine failure during Glasgow Fair and **Glenmore** had to be hurriedly chartered from John Williamson to deputise for her. On yet another occasion her electricity system failed and she returned to her base with emergency oil lighting illuminating her way.

During the following close season she had a substantial overhaul. The saloons were refurnished, new steam steering was fitted, the main mast was removed and the welldeck covered over, so that the promenade deck formed one continuous line with the level of the forecastle. The deck below the new extension, however, was not plated in. A bowsprit was added, and with her funnel changed to red she was ready for a fresh start. Unfortunately her performance was not improved and eventually, with the threat of the turbine era in the air, Williamson's **Strathmore** took over the Campbeltown route.

Under the flag of Clyde Excursion Steamers Ltd. she assumed her third name, **Carrick Castle,** and was based at Glasgow, giving an assortment of cruises from the Broomielaw. She was also open for charter work and in August, 1899, took part in an unusual excursion from Campbeltown to the Isle of Man. **Carrick Castle** conveyed the trippers on the first leg of their journey from Campbeltown to Stranraer, where they entrained for Garlieston, sailing the rest of the way to Douglas in the Isle of Man Steam Packet's boat **Prince of Wales**.

The following year proved to be **Carrick Castle's** last on the Clyde. M. T. Clark was now managing her and she was engaged mostly in making runs to the Kyles of Bute. This final season was indeed a short one, only from the Queen's Birthday Holiday until early August. Then she proceeded to Govan Dry Dock for strengthening in order to face the winds and waves beyond the Clyde. Her new masters were the Russian-owned Chinese Eastern Railway and her new headquarters were at Port Arthur under yet another new title, **Nagadan.**

When the Russo-Japanese war broke out in 1904 she was used as a fleet auxiliary. The Japanese troops advanced with such rapidity that they thwarted an attempt to blow up the **Nagadan** and she was captured intact. After the war she ran under the Japanese flag, first as **Nagara Maru** and later as **Tenri Maru.** In November 1931, she went ashore at Matsu Shima, Japan. This may well have been the swansong of a Clyde passenger steamer which somehow never quite made the grade.

G.S.

P.S. 'JUNO'

J. NICHOLSON.

P.S. Juno

The last addition to the Glasgow and South Western fleet before the turn of the century was **Juno** from the Clydebank Shipbuilding and Engineering Company. Some mystery surrounds her introduction into the railway ranks. In the 1890's new vessels destined for the Firth received a wheen of publicity right from the laying down of the keel, yet **Juno** made her debut almost unheralded. Not until the last days of June, 1898, did a small paragraph appear in the Press announcing that the new paddle steamer completing at Clydebank was named **Juno** and would run for the G. & S.W. Rumour has it that she was originally intended for the South Coast and came to the Clyde services, in a manner of speaking, secondhand.

Juno was a big vessel by Clyde standards, with a girth that fitted her for work in any weather. Her powerful engines could drive her at over 19 knots, as she proved on her trials over the Skelmorlie mile on July 5, 1898.

Juno was also one of the first Clyde passenger boats to be demobbed, and was a useful asset to the scanty fleet operating in the initial post-war summer when she maintained the Rothesay and Kyles of Bute service for the G. & S.W. Her first run was made on June 28 after a speedy reconditioning at Barclay Curle's yard. Soon she was back to her old haunt of Ayr, but no longer cruised to Stranraer as in pre-war days.

Her first call was at Rothesay three days later with a party of Greenock excursionists bound for Ayr, and thenceforth she made Ayr her base. This gave her all too few opportunities to display her prowess as a racer unless she encountered a rival on some of her cruises up Firth to the Gareloch, Loch Long, Rothesay or the Kyles of Bute. Much of her sailing was done towards Arran and she made weekly trips to Stranraer, where she remained overnight while her passengers returned by rail.

Juno was really a summer "butterfly boat" although she occasionally filled in during spring and autumn (while some of her colleagues were overhauling) by running from Princes Pier. Because of her weatherly qualities **Juno** was the first Clyde enlistment to the white ensign when war was declared in 1914. She served from February, 1915, until April, 1919, under the rather misleading title of **H.M.S. Junior.**

Her proud record of freedom from mishap ended in July, 1920, when she broke two brackets in her paddlewheel a mile south of Ailsa Craig. With the assistance of the tug at Ayr she was taken back to port and later up Firth.

In 1913 she came under L.M.S. control and it was not long before her graceful grey hull had been changed to black and the red base of her tall, slightly elliptical funnel turned to buff.

Most of the South Western boats were rather notorious for their coal consumption and, as such, were none too popular with their new London managers. **Glen Sannox** had already been withdrawn from service when, in 1931, the economy axe terminated the career of the big, beamy, beautiful **Juno**. She made her last run on September 12 and the following February was sent to Alloa for breaking up.

G.S.

P.S. Duchess of Fife

To augment their fleet, the Caledonian Steam Packet Company in 1902 had the paddle steamer **Duchess of Montrose** built for them by John Brown's. She was a pretty little ship, of a handy pattern that made her ideal for all-the-year-round work, but of only moderate pace. The following year the C.S.P. Company required a duplicate order, so pleased had they been with their latest acquisition. Whether through pressure of other business at Clydebank, I know not, but the contract finally went to Fairfield.

This was actually the first Clyde passenger steamer constructed in the Govan yard and so successful were the builders that one is tempted to think that the order was long overdue.

Fairfield turned out a really splendid job, very similar to the "Duchess" of the previous year, and even managed to coax an extra knot or two through the finely balanced ratio of hull line and engine power.

The year 1903 saw **Duchess of Fife**, as the new boat was called, sally forth to join the "other titled ladies of Gourock". Originally she possessed a surprising turn of speed that enabled her to compete, often successfully, with higher powered craft and, as a winter boat, she was the essence of efficiency.

Her life started on the Rothesay section with its attendant afternoon cruise to the Kyles of Bute, but so versatile was the "wee Fife" that she had been known to deputise even for the turbine **Queen Alexandra** on the Campbeltown route.

She saw service in both world wars. In the first she was exclusively used as a minesweeper and was based in Grimsby, but in the second her naval duties were more varied. As a unit of the 12th Minesweeping Flotilla she was in company with the other Clyde favourites **Waverley**, **Marmion** and **Eagle III** and helped to succour the beleaguered forces on the Dunkirk beaches. Convoy and ferry duties followed before she was ready to resume her peacetime role.

Her first job on her return was on the Holy Loch run. Unfortunately her engine seized up as she lay at Kilmun on the afternoon schedule and her passengers were returned to Gourock via bus to Dunoon and then by another steamer. Thereafter she became associated with the Wemyss Bay- Largs- Millport and Kilchattan Bay route till the close of her illustrious career in June, 1953. She was broken up at Port Glasgow in the autumn of that year.

Apart from going ashore in dense fog near Kirn in 1936 her career was entirely free from incident, which was a fine record for a vessel which saw Clyde service in and out of season.

The changeover in the Clyde fleet to diesel driven Maids and car ferries was the swan song of the little **Duchess of Fife**, a vessel which had rightly earned the designation " the ideal hull model and design for a Clyde passenger steamer."

G.S.

P.S. Marmion

After the North British had launched their most outstanding vessel, **Waverley**, at the close of the 19th century, seven years were to elapse before there was an addition to the ranks. Then came **Marmion**, from the same yard, A. and J. Inglis at Pointhouse. She was more or less a smaller and less powerful version of her famous predecessor. Again the foresaloon was carried well forward of the mast, with a short low bow. The only appreciable difference in general outline was the arrangement of the bridge foward of the funnel instead of between the paddleboxes.

With her well raked red, white and black funnel, a lavish application of gilt for adornment and a general neatness of design, she was altogether most pleasing to the eye. Internally, too, **Marmion** was a big advance on anything that had appeared at Craigendoran, in fact her well designed furnishings were never bettered in a Clyde steamer.

March 12, 1906, saw the new boat running her trials on the Gareloch measured mile where she clocked 17.3 knots, not a great speed, but the excessive demands for pace that had prevailed in the nineties no longer held. She then embarked on a cruise up and down Lochs Long and Goil, skirted Dunoon, Innellan and Toward and on to the Kyles of Bute before returning to headquarters.

She replaced **Redgauntlet** on the Arrochar cruise and gave the Holy Loch commuters a morning and evening service. This routine was followed until 1915 when, in April, she was called for naval duties as a minesweeper. For this service the Admiralty altered her considerably, extending the promenade deck to the bow and plating in the hull,

After a fairly uneventful career under the white ensign she returned to the Clyde for the 1920 season. The structural alterations carried out for war service were retained but they had affected her trim and greatly impaired her handling at piers.

Marmion was on the Arrochar run once more until the reappearance of **Waverley** in July, when she was transferred to the Rothesay route. At the end of the summer she retired to Bowling Harbour and did not re-emerge until 1926. By then the fleet was sailing under the L.N.E.R. flag, and she replaced **Dandie Dinmont,** which

eventually went to the Hull-New Holland car ferry service. **Marmion** came out to rejoin her colleagues with her foresaloon considerably shortened (it barely reached beyond the bridge) and, if she was no longer the "beauty queen" of her youth, she was once again a most seaworthy vessel.

She went on to the Dunoon and Rothesay run, with an afternoon cruise to the Kyles of Bute thrown in and, with her stability regained, was usually the L.N.E.R. winter boat.

In 1932 she was considerably altered internally. The main saloon was gutted, to be replaced by a combination of cocktail lounge, tearoom and tiny alcove fitted with basket chairs-modern, but lacking the warmth of the older type saloon.

The year 1936 found the Craigendoran boats adopting a new livery of grey hulls and white upperworks and **Marmion** was one of the first to turn out in the new colour scheme. Although the Bute service was her customary route she made occasional jaunts to Loch Long and Loch Goil, and in 1938 was a frequent visitor to Largs.

Marmion had a wonderfully placid existence as a pleasure craft. In all her years of service I recall only one incident out of the ordinary. This occurred in Rothesay Bay when she was lying out at the company moorings. She suffered the indignity of being rammed by a yacht and holed by its bowsprit, fortunately well above the waterline.

Taken for another spell of war duty in 1939 she was once again similarly reconstructed, but the good fortune that had attended her in the First World War now deserted her. She survived the holocaust of Dunkirk, where she added to the glory of the little ships, but was bombed and sunk at Harwich in April, 1941, in shallow water.

So passed from the scene the bonnie wee **Marmion**, the last vessel to join the fleet of the old North British Railway Company.

G.S.

P.S. "EAGLE III"   J. NICHOLSON.

P.S. Eagle III

In 1910 the name **Eagle** cropped up again in Buchanan's fleet list, but this time suffixed by the Roman numeral III. The new boat was in actual fact the fourth **Eagle** to have been either built or bought for the company. In 1852 the first one appeared under the Buchanan houseflag and ran for 10 years before being sold for blockade running during the American Civil War. Number two was laid down to replace her but, before she was launched, the lure of gold proved too tempting and she, too, made her exit from the Clyde for the other side of the Atlantic. Only a year elapsed before the third was in the water and Buchanans had the use of her right up to 1892, when she went to the Manchester Ship Canal.

Eagle III was ordered from A. & J. Inglis, who subcontracted the building of the hull to Napier & Miller. Required for the all-the-way sailings, great speed was not imperative, nor were her internal decorations of the high standard of the crack railway boats of the period. An economical steamer capable of moderate pace was what Buchanan ordered and certainly **Eagle III** was all that.

On the first day of June, 1910, the new ship duly appeared on the Clyde, sporting the black funnel with white band, but right from the start of her career it was apparent that there was a defect somewhere in her hull construction. With anything like a reasonable crowd aboard she listed to an alarming degree. As a result, long before the season closed, her name suddenly vanished from the Buchanan advertisements in the daily press . . . **Eagle III** had gone back to the builders for modifications. She reappeared in 1911 completely cured of her ailment.

Long will she be remembered as the 11 o'clock boat from the Broomielaw for Dunoon, Rothesay and the Kyles of Bute with the full day's sail (including dinner and plain tea) at a cost of 4s. 6d. She alternated her Kyles cruise with ones to the head of Loch Striven or round the Island of Cumbrae.

The Admiralty claimed her for minesweeping work out of Grimsby and Harwich during the First World War, and before she returned she was also engaged in conveying food between Britain and Holland.

As built her navigating bridge had been placed between the paddle boxes but when reconditioned this was moved to forward of the funnel. A solid awning which covered part of her after deck was not replaced but in its stead there appeared a small upper deck over her after companionway.

By now, the old Clyde firm of Buchanan had amalgamated with the equally well established one of Williamson and, as a unit of the Williamson - Buchanan fleet, **Eagle III** funnel colouring was changed to white with black top. The end of March, 1920, saw her back on her old route but the cost for the day's outing had doubled since before the war.

In 1933 she was ousted from her popular sailing time by the transference of **King Edward** to the up-river fleet. Three years later the fleet had come under the Caledonian Steam Packet Company, and **Eagle III** appeared on a number of runs on railway connections at the coast termini. Later part of her weekly schedule was spent on the Loch Goil route.

She was conscripted again for white ensign work in the 1939-45 war and served as **H.M.S. Oriole**. During the Dunkirk evacuation she was grounded on the beach there, and thousands made their getaway via her decks while she acted the role of a temporary landing stage.

Eagle III was by no means a veteran, as Clyde steamers go, when she returned to her native river, but her boiler was in need of replacement. The absence of a firm capable of producing the now outmoded haystack variety is said to have been the cause of her not returning to active Clyde service. After lying for some time in the Holy Loch she was towed to Port Glasgow and there broken up in 1946.

G.S.

P.S. Jeanie Deans

At the beginning of 1923, the originators of the Craigendoran route to the coast, the North British, lost their identity in the London and North Eastern grouping in the railway amalgamations. The fleet remained unaltered for eight years before being enlarged by the addition of a new vessel, **Jeanie Deans**. On April 7, 1931, a daughter of Mr. William Whitelaw, then chairman of the L.N.E.R., named the new boat at the Fairfield yard.

She was the second vessel to bear this name. Her predecessor, built almost half a century earlier, was one of the outstanding ships of her era and did much to bring the Craigendoran fleet to the forefront. The new vessel did nothing to besmirch that record. She was the biggest vessel to appear on this route — 258 ft. long, 30 ft. beam, 839 gross tons — and in her original guise sported two rather stumpy funnels which somehow did not altogether lend themselves to a ship of her length, smart though she undoubtedly looked. The shortness of the funnels was also the cause of much cinder being showered on her decks, unless the wind was blowing strongly from abeam. As a result "**Jeanie**" appeared in her second season with the "lums" heightened but unfortunately not to an equal degree. The cinder menace had been removed but aesthetically her outline had been sadly marred.

After war service, **Jeanie Deans** reappeared in June, 1946, with yet another pair of funnels... elliptical and of greater girth and, it might be added, more in keeping with her dimensions.

As built, **Jeanie Deans'** promenade deck was almost completely unhampered but, in 1932, she was given observation lounges fore and aft and these, after her spell on naval duty, were covered over to the full width of the vessel, although only the after one was allocated to passenger accommodation.

The L.N.E.R. retained the old N.B. livery of black hull, brown deck structures and red, white and black funnel. In 1936 there was a change when the hull became light grey and the deck buildings white.

Jeanie Deans sampled all these changes and then donned the more austere colouring of the nationalised fleets in 1948.

The original after-saloon was a thing of beauty, with light oak woodwork and rose pink furnishings. This was later converted into the main dining saloon previously located on a lower deck.

Plenty of power was evident in the engine room, where her three crank diagonal machinery drove her at a speed in excess of 18 knots on her trials, a pace which stamped her, like her predecessor, as one of the fastest paddle boats of her time.

The first duty of **Jeanie Deans** was on the Arrochar run in connection with the Loch Lomond tour. Then she essayed an assortment of cruises from Helensburgh and Craigendoran which took her to and round Arran, around Ailsa Craig, and to Ayr and Girvan.

After war service she was for a spell on the Kyles of Bute run, later on the round Bute cruise. She closed her Clyde career by alternating week about with **Waverley** on the Arrochar and round Bute stations.

On war service she had been both mine sweeper and anti-aircraft defence vessel and she narrowly escaped destruction during the London blitz from a land mine which accounted for the Clyde steamer **Juno.**

At the end of the 1964 season **Jeanie Deans** was laid up in Albert Harbour, Greenock, her services no longer required because of the policy of reduction in the Clyde flotilla. She was bought by a consortium of English business men who sailed her south. Her departure from the Clyde scene removed not only a popular paddleboat but, probably, the best loved pleasure steamer of recent years.

Renamed **Queen of the South**, she sailed intermittently on the Thames in 1966 but, despite the expenditure of large sums of money including the fitting of a bow rudder, the 1967 season was a disaster. She was towed to Antwerp for scrapping.

G.S.&I.M.

P.S. 'CALEDONIA'   J. NICHOLSON

P.S. Caledonia

Denny of Dumbarton turned out, in 1934, their first paddle steamer for the Clyde passenger fleet since they had launched the famous **Duchess of Hamilton** in 1890. The reason for the new tonnage was the departure to the breakers of two old faithfuls, **Caledonia** and **Mercury**, which had figured in the original building programmes of the Caledonian and Glasgow and South Western fleets respectively.

The replacements were also paddle driven and assumed the same titles, but here the similarity ended. In external design the new **Caledonia** and her quasi-sister **Mercury** (building at Fairfield) were revolutionary types for the river. They had twin masts, elliptical funnels, observation lounges on the promenade deck with passenger accommodation atop, and flying bridges which protruded beyond the breadth of the hulls. Cruiser sterns were also adopted.

Perhaps the most startling change was in the design of the paddleboxes. Gone were the lovely curve offline and the symmetrical vents and decorative embellishments. In their place there was a rectangular box-like affair on deck while the choke escapes were paced apart like saloon windows. Indeed it was somewhat difficult to distinguish the new craft as "sidewheelers" when viewing them from a distance on the beam.

Below deck was another novelty; the cabin dining saloon was placed in the position normally occupied by the saloon. Below that there was a tea room and smoke room. With a capacity of 1,300 passengers, **Caledonia** was a roomy, comfortable and most efficient vessel.

After topping 17 knots on the Skelmorlie mile, **Caledonia** came into service on March 31, the Saturday of the Glasgow Spring Holiday, and special handbills were produced to entice the travelling public to sample the new boats on their initial runs. **Caledonia** was on the Gourock and Wemyss Bay connections to Dunoon, Rothesay and the Kyles and proved herself a worthy vessel.

During the ensuing summer she ran short cruises from Largs and Millport and in her first off-season helped out with the winter services. Two years later she replaced **Duchess of Argyll** in summer on the Arran route via the Kyles of Bute, and was quite often seen up-river at week-ends on cruises from Bridge Wharf.

Caledonia was commissioned for war service in December, 1939, and played her part as minesweeper and flak ship in the Dover Patrol, the Battle of Britain, the Normandy D-Day landings, the relief of Antwerp and the Battle of the V Bombs. On Christmas Eve, 1940, she was on patrol with **Mercury** off the south-east corner of Ireland when the latter hit a mine. For four hours **Caledonia** laboured to tow the stricken ship back to port but **Mercury** sank some miles out from Milford Haven.

Caledonia arrived back on the Clyde in May, 1945, but it was 12 months before she resumed her peace-time duties.

After her return she played many roles on the Clyde coast scene. She made railway connections from all the coastal termini, performed the Arran and Cambeltown cruises as well as the trip round the Island of Bute, and was the Ayr based excursion steamer from 1954 to 1964. From 1965 to 1969 she succeeded **Jeannie Deans** as one of the two Craigendorn based paddlers and then her grand finale was on the Royal Route in succession to **Lochfyne.**

Caledonia was the first of the Clyde paddlers to be converted to oil burning when the Railway Executive decided to adopt this fuel. (Back in the 'nineties Captain Williamson had tried oil fuel in her predecessor but with mixed results and she was soon back on coal.)

Not all the exciting episodes of **Caledonia**'s career were confined to the war years. Before she donned navy grey she and **Duchess of Argyll** were in collision at Gourock. Then in December 1953, her engines broke down off Innellan on the 10.25 morning up run from Rothesay and she had to drop anchor. A tug eventually towed her to Wemyss Bay. In her latter years she had a more tranquil existence, though on one occasion **Glen Sannox** had to come to her assistance when she had an engine failure in Millport Bay.

She ended her years as a floating restaurant on the Thames under the name of **Old Caledonia** until destroyed by fire in 1980.

G.S.&I.M.

D.E.P.V. 'TALISMAN' in 1935.   J. NICHOLSON.

─── D.E.P.V. Talisman ───

On April 14, 1935, Miss Evelyn Whitelaw, daughter of the Chairman of the London and North Eastern Railway Company, named a new vessel **Talisman** at Inglis' yard at Pointhouse. This was a replacement for the old North British vessel of the same name which had been condemned to the breaker's hammers at Barrow.

Only in name did she bear any resemblance to her predecessor. She was, in many ways, quite a revolutionary ship. Heating, cooking, mooring winches and steering were all electric, but possibly the outstanding feature was the paddlewheels driven by an electric drum powered by diesel motors placed forward on the lower deck.

Happily the designers did not resort to the "disguised paddlebox" cult which had crept into the Clyde fleet the previous year, but **Talisman** was given a none too graceful hull and an ugly cruiser stern, while the customary rail forward was replaced by a solid bulwark. The single funnel was flat-sided and had a quaint gadget, for all the world like a giant tiddlywink, on top, "to cut out the noise of the diesels," it was said. Unfortunately it did not.

The rapidity with which **Talisman** could be pressed into service, as compared with her steam driven sisters, was a mark in her favour, and a further item on the credit side was the fact that her engines could be controlled directly from the bridge.

In the first week of June she did her trials, clocking over 17 knots, and on Saturday the 11th she made her service debut, taking her place on the L.N.E.R. timetable from Craigendoran, making the early Rothesay connection and the afternoon excursion to the Kyles of Bute. She proved an efficient timekeeper with sufficient in reserve to make up any arrears in schedule. At piers, however, she was none too handy and, with the way off her, was apt to lie like a log in the water, requiring much assistance from her mooring capstans when berthing.

When the L.N.E.R drastically cut their service in 1939 to three vessels, **Talisman** became a mere ferryboat to Dunoon and Rothesay.

Then came the war, and she was taken over by the Admiralty in the late summer of 1940. After conversion to a ship of war at Pointhouse, she emerged as the incongruously titled **H.M.S. Aristocrat**. Her first naval duties took her to Methil as a Bofors gun defence vessel and then she moved south to become one of the Thames Local Defence flotilla.

Eventually a more peaceful anchorage was found when, in company with **Royal Eagle**, she headed for Loch-na-Keal where preparations were going ahead for the North Africa landings. Back once more to the Thames, she was based at Sheerness and worked between there, Newhaven and the Dorset coast where raiding manoeuvres were carried out. When D Day came **H M.S. Aristocrat** was H.Q. Ship at Mulberry Harbour, when she sustained damage to her bow which necessitated her return to Portsmouth for repairs.

Talisman was back on the Clyde for the 1946 season. Gone was the solid bulwark, replaced by an open rail, and a main mast had been added. In the company of **Jeanie Deans** and **Lucy Ashton** she resumed the Craigendoran sailings to Rothesay.

In 1947 the Clyde fleet was nationalised and **Talisman's** tri-colour funnel of red, white and black eventually gave way to the drab buff.

She was kept on as winter boat, minus overhaul, and soon earned the unenviable title of "the slow boat to Rothesay." Public protest was so strong that **Waverley** was brought out to replace her.

An overhaul of some magnitude was now overdue and, after it, she emerged for the 1954 season as the Millport boat, on which run she remained with distinction.

During the 1967 off-season she was withdrawn from service awaiting a buyer, and her loss to the Cumbrae may be measured by the fact that, for the first time, sailing tickets were required for this run during Glasgow Fair in July, because of the inability of the Maids to deputise capably in her absence.

G.S.

P.S. "JUPITER"   J. NICHOLSON.

P.S. Jupiter

Something new in profile was added to the Clyde scene in 1937, when the Fairfield yard launched from the same slipway two almost identical paddleboats for the London Midland and Scottish fleet. These were **Juno** (lost in the London blitz of 1941) and **Jupiter.**

This pair were given deck observation lounges, concealed type paddleboxes and twin masts, features which had been introduced during this decade, but unlike the other paddleboats of the flotilla they sported two funnels.

Of pleasing design, in spite of the attempt to disguise the fact that she was a paddle steamer, **Jupiter** somehow never quite attained the speed of her twin. She was, nevertheless, with her great beam and space amidships, a grand passenger and goods carrier and a most useful member of the fleet.

Her career began on the Dunoon-Rothesay-Kyles of Bute service and, after an uneventful opening spell, she ran into trouble while on her first winter duty. In attempting to take Millport (not always the most pleasant of tasks in winter time) she was caught by the southerly swell and rammed the pier to a depth of several feet. When, in the following June, she was in collision with several yachts moored off Hunter's Quay one would be tempted to believe that she was rather slow in answering to the helm. Her episodes extraordinary were not concluded until she had gone ashore near Brodick during a particularly thick fog.

Having got over her youthful adventures she settled down and was one of the first vessels to be called to Admiralty duty in the war. As **H.M.S.Scawfell** she served with distinction as a minesweeper in the Clyde area and later at Milford Haven, Portland and Dover. After a period as an anti-aircraft unit on the east coast convoy routes, she was in the thick of the battle during the Normandy landings.

She was the first Clyde steamer to return to peace-time work and went on to the Holy Loch run in February 1946. During the summer she returned to give a modified version of her Dunoon and Rothesay trading. When the car ferries made their debut, **Jupiter** was relegated to the role of assistant steamer on the Wemyss Bay-Rothesay run. She also became identified with the Cumbrae Circle Cruise and made occasional sailings from Ayr and from the Bridge Wharf to Lochgoil.

Having been converted from coal burning to oil fuel early in 1957, it was rather surprising to find her taken out of service and laid up in Albert Harbour, Greenock, the same year. Finally in April, 1961, she departed for the shipbreaker's in Dublin. So passed just about the most pleasing design of the dwindling Clyde paddle fleet.

G.S.

P.S. "WAVERLEY" in 1948

J. NICHOLSON.

P.S. Waverley

On 29th May 1940, the LNER's paddle steamer **Waverley,** of 1899, was bombed and lost while returning to England from the beaches of Dunkirk loaded with troops. After the war the LNER was left with only **Jeanie Deans** of 1931, **Talisman** of 1935 and **Lucy Ashton** of 1888. Both **Jeanie Deans** and **Talisman** had been requisitioned by the Admiralty and were in need of extensive overhauls. Single handed, and without a proper overhaul for six and a half years, **Lucy Ashton** had performed all L.N.E.R.'S wartime services out of its headquarters at Craigendoran. After the war the L.N.E.R. was, therefore, desperate for new tonnage.

To succeed **Lucy Ashton** a new vessel was built in 1946, and in memory of the vessel lost at Dunkirk was given the name **Waverley**. **Waverley,** which went into service in 1947, did not arouse any particular interest when new. She could have been built fifty years previously. The only outward concession to modernity were raked stem, funnels and masts and a cruiser stern, yet **Waverley** is now known the length and breadth of the British Isles as the last sea going paddle streamer in the world. Not that the LNER had built **Waverley** to ply beyond the confines of the Firth of Clyde, but events since have taken her regularly to the Western Isles, the Irish Sea, the North Wales coast, the Bristol Channel, the English Channel, the Thames and even to Dunkirk.

Waverley emerged in traditional L.N.E.R. colours right down to brown deckhouses and, with her rebuilt consorts **Jeanie Deans** and **Talisman** and the old **Lucy Ashton,** provided a splash of colour to a drab post-war Clyde. The ripples from the splash were to be short lived for, with nationalisation of the railways, all the railway steamers adopted the drab buff and black of B.R. It was not long before the brown deckhouses became white as did the paddle boxes. However, **Waverley** found her way from the upper Firth to Arran and Campbeltown and also went upriver to Glasgow. In 1965 B.R.'s new corporate colour scheme appeared. On the Clyde, hulls became monastral blue and a red lion was fitted to the sides of the funnels. **Waverley's** lions, like most of the others, were out of proportion. Then in 1973 the S.T.G., **Waverley's** new owners, applied their new Caledonian MacBrayne colours. Once again, **Waverley** looked the part with black hull and paddle boxes, and red funnels with yellow disks round the lions which appeared to have grown in stature. Despite efforts to promote their last paddler, the S.T.G. withdrew her from service after the 1973 summer season.

By 1975 her new owners, Waverley Steam Navigation Company - a subsidiary of P.S.P.S. - had **Waverley** in steam again and back in her L.N.E.R. funnel colours. Since then, despite a grounding, having to be reboilered and having to get her paddle wheels rebuilt, **Waverley** has gone from strength to strength.

I.M.

S.S. Davaar

To replace a paddle steamer called **Gael**, which had gone south to join the Great Western Railway fleet, the Campbeltown and Glasgow Steam Packet Joint Stock Company had **Davaar** built in 1885 by the London and Glasgow Shipbuilding Yard at Govan.

The Campbeltown company had been in the shipping business since 1826. All their vessels had been paddle driven until 1869, when **Kintyre** started the vogue of screw propulsion and yacht-like hull design, even down to the bowsprit. **Kinloch** followed the same pattern 10 years later and **Davaar** carried on the tradition, which was to end with her demise.

Davaar possessed only moderate speed but made up for this deficiency by her seaworthiness which was a necessity for her all-the-year-round duties. The Kilbrannan Sound could be a dirty stretch of water in the winter months.

As built, **Davaar** had two rather thin funnels set close together, but when reboilered in 1903 a single funnel of greater diameter was fitted, a change which enhanced her appearance. At this time, too, the main saloon aft, which had alleyways down each side, was widened to the full breadth of the ship. The promenade deck above the saloon was extended to the stern, but the side plating terminated with the saloon, leaving approximately some 15 feet at the rear open to the elements.

With **Kintyre** and **Kinloch** using the Glasgow terminal, **Davaar**, maintained a daily service to Campbeltown from Custom House Quay, Greenock, with calls at Princes Pier, Gourock, Lochranza, Pirnmill, Carradale and Saddell until 1907 when **Kintyre** was lost off Skelmorlie. **Davaar** then went up river to join **Kinloch**.

Twelve years earlier, **Davaar** herself had all but broken up the partnership of the "three graceful sisters". Since the earliest days the townsfolk of Campbeltown had enjoyed a bi-annual excursion to Belfast and on June 7 1895, **Davaar** was on this run. On entering Belfast Lough she ran into dense fog and grounded on a rocky stretch of the coastline known as Brigg's Reef. All the passengers were taken ashore safely but when the tide dropped **Davaar**'s bows were left rearing high in the air and she was in danger of breaking her back. But she proved a stout craft and was successfully refloated after two days of anxiety and suspense. One of the rescue tugs sent to her assistance was not so fortunate, running over a submerged wreck and sinking.

Davaar returned to her route in less than a week and sailed for the rest of her career as consort to **Kinloch** and later to **Dalriada.**

During the 1914-18 war she continued on the Campbeltown service, running for a short period in 1915 from Ardrossan as base, and latterly from Wemyss Bay because of the submarine defence boom at Dunoon.

In 1937 a change in ownership in the Clyde and Campbeltown Company saw the familiar black funnel with broad red band give place to one of red with a black top.

In the Second World War, with the threat of invasion in 1940, **Davaar** sailed south for Newhaven, where she was to be sunk as a blockship at the harbour entrance. Fortunately this did not become necessary, but she never again raised steam. When the danger had passed she was beached on the Sussex coast and scrapped in 1943.

G.S.

T.S. "KING EDWARD" J. NICHOLSON

Tr.S.S King Edward

The service to Campbeltown had been, for many years, in the hands of the local concern, the Campbeltown and Glasgow Steam Packet Joint Stock Company, when in the nineties a boat called the **Herald** made daily runs from Fairlie; later another paddleboat, **Culzean Castle** appeared on the same route. There had also been odd day excursions to the Kintyre capital by a host of other Clyde pleasure steamers but towards the close of the century the Williamsons decided to compete for this traffic. Their paddle steamer **Strathmore** was put on the run, but she was only a pro tem stand-in for a revolutionary new vessel which was shortly to make her debut.. a turbine propelled craft. There had been screw vessels before in the Clyde fleet, but they had all been driven by reciprocating engines.

Sir Charles Parsons had so successfully demonstrated the merits of his invention with his experimental ship **Turbinia** that the Admiralty ordered two new destroyers to be turbine powered, but when **King Edward** appeared on the Clyde she was the first commercial turbine-driven ship in the world.

In 1901 Denny of Dumbarton launched the new Turbine Steamers Syndicate boat. Her attractive appearance and her speed of more than 20 knots, coupled with the smoothness of her running, made her an instant success. Below decks she was fitted out in the conventional manner of the paddle steamer of her day, although the public missed the thrilling sight of whirling cranks when "visiting the engines."

So effective was she on service that the following year another and larger turbine, **Queen Alexandra**, appeared on the scene and a new route had to be worked out for the pioneer. By 1902 she was sailing via Dunoon, Fairlie and Rothesay to Tarbert and Ardrishaig round the Garroch Head. Later her run was extended to Inveraray. Here she clashed with the well established **Lord of the Isles**, but eventually forced the old paddleboat off the route.

After successful work as a troopship in the English Channel in the First World War, she was kitted out as a hospital ship for a run to Archangel. Her return voyage from Russia was a perilous one owing to the extreme stress of weather, and she docked at Aberdeen many days overdue.

Peacetime found her back on the Campbeltown run, from which she deviated rarely until, with the advent of **King George V** in 1926, she came up river to join the Williamson-Buchanan "all the way" fleet.

King Edward's adventures did not end with her war-time experiences. In July, 1925, she was run into by **Duchess of Argyll** off Largs and escaped possible foundering by the stoutness of the belting round her hull.

Although remaining in home waters throughout the period of the Second World War, she had another alarming experience when a collision with **Lairdsburn** resulted in a great hole being torn in her bow. Later, in the late forties, she was an innocent but unfortunate bystander when a tow rope between a tug and a large cargo vessel was accidentally swept across her foredeck, snapping off her mast.

By this time she was a unit of the nationalised Clyde fleet and was frequently pressed into service for railway connections at the coast termini.

Shortly after celebrating her golden jubilee, **King Edward** was withdrawn from service and taken to Troon for breaking up.

The estuary lost a notable vessel with the passing of this old favourite. In an era which has witnessed the rise and dominance of the diesel engine with its attendant noise and vibration, her tranquillity of motion would have been all the more pronounced for, despite her age, **King Edward's** machinery appeared to be running as smoothly as the day she pioneered turbine propulsion on the Clyde.

G.S.

Tr.S.S. Duchess of Argyll

To counter the success of the first two turbine steamers, **King Edward** and **Queen Alexandra** which had been built in 1901 and 1902 for Turbine Steamers, the Caledonian Steam Packet Company had an unnamed turbine steamer built in 1906 by the same builders, Denny of Dumbarton. The vessel was subsequently named **Duchess of Argyll**. Although identical in size and very similar in general layout to **King Edward**, **Duchess of Argyll** followed the Caledonian pattern of having her forward mooring gear on her main deck which was open at the bow. Unlike the two earlier turbines, the forward saloon on the main deck had windows in line with the Caledonian paddlers. As the vessel was earmarked for the Ardrossan to Arran route, she was fitted with a bow rudder for manoeuvering in the confines of the mainland port. The Glasgow and South Western Railway's vessel on the run was shown a clear pair of heels.

After only three years in service, **Duchess of Argyll** was laid up in 1909 as part of a pooling arrangement which was reached between the Caledonian and the Glasgow and South Western Railway to rationalise services and reduce losses. Speed and duplication of services did not come cheaply even in those days.

In 1910, to improve her sea keeping qualities, **Duchess of Argyll's** forward saloon windows were replaced by portholes and the mooring deck was plated up. This was to enable the **Argyll** to be chartered to the operators of the Stranraer-Larne service for relief work on that exposed crossing. Her one and only stint on the North Channel was in June 1911 as a result of the mail steamer **Princess Maud** damaging her bow at Larne.

Normality returned until the Great War. Initially the **Argyll** was not affected but then, in February 1915, she and her consorts **Duchess of Montrose** and **Duchess of Hamilton** were all requisitioned as transports. The **Argyll's** arena of service was the English Channel, which she crossed 655 times between her call up and her release in April 1919. In 1917 the Williamson steamer **Queen Empress**, which was also serving as a transport, was in collision with its destroyer escort and towed into Boulogne by the **Argyll.**

With the cessation of hostilities, the **Argyll** returned to the Clyde. Initially she served Rothesay and Dunoon but, after a refit in the

Spring of 1920, she took up the Arran run again, albeit out of Princes Pier and Gourock and via the Kyles of Bute. In 1922 the **Argyll** was again earmarked as relief vessel for Stranraer-Larne and for this purpose she was fitted with wireless telegraphy. In the event she was not required.

1923 saw the grouping of the railways and the repainting of the **Argyll's** handsome yellow funnels in the instantly unpopular "tartan" format of yellow and red band and black top. After two years the red band was dropped.

In 1936 the **Argyll** again changed her route, sailing from Gourock to Inveraray on Mondays, Wednesdays and Fridays and to Campbeltown on Tuesdays, Thursdays and Saturdays. The Inveraray service provided one half of the popular circular Loch Eck tour.

On the outbreak of war in September 1939 the **Argyll's** cruises were cancelled, as were all the others. Within days, the **Argyll** was back on her original route from Ardrossan to Arran. From November 1939 Fairlie became the port for Arran, with sailings often being round the north end of Cumbrae and round the south of Holy Isle into Lamlash. Shortly thereafter, the **Argyll** moved up-Firth to the Gourock - Dunoon run and latterly again served as a transport, albeit only to troopships moored at the Tail of the Bank.

With victory, the boom was dismantled, and sailings from the upper Firth piers to those below the boom were again possible. The **Argyll** took the first post war sailing from Gourock to Rothesay. Thereafter the **Argyll**, now forty years old, was demoted to the more leisurely mid-day Kyles of Bute service from Princes Pier and Gourock. Although she acquired a wheel house, the long years of war had taken their toll on the **Argyll's** accommodation. 1951 was, however, to be her last year on the Clyde, and it was therefore fitting that on Fridays she gave an extra service run to Arran via the Kyles and on Saturday afternoon, after a forenoon on the upper Firth, she served Arran from Wemyss Bay.

Although her sailing days were over, the **Argyll** was not scrapped until 1970. She was purchased by the Admiralty in 1952 and, after being stripped, served as a floating laboratory at the Underwater Detection Establishment at Portland Harbour.

I.M.

R.M.S. "SAINT COLUMBA"   J. NICHOLSON. 1962.

Tr.S.S. Saint Columba

Turbine Steamers' second turbine, **Queen Alexandra,** followed closely on the heels of **King Edward,** such was the success of the pioneering vessel. **Queen Alexandra's** time on the Clyde was, however, to be short lived as she suffered fire damage in 1911 and was sold to Canadian Pacific Railway Co who had her repaired by her builders - Denny of Dumbarton - renamed her **Princess Patricia** and sailed her to British Columbia via Cape Horn. She plied on the west coast of Canada until she was broken up in 1937.

Meanwhile, to take her place on the Clyde, Turbine Steamers had Denny build an almost identical replacement which was also named **Queen Alexandra**. The principal differences were the provision of additional astern power and a bow rudder. The first **Queen Alexandra** started the shade deck which was repeated in the replacement vessel and was added subsequently to **King Edward** and repeated in many later vessels.

Queen Alexandra was built with scantlings sufficient for an all year round passenger certificate between Ardrossan and Campbeltown, and it was on the Upper Firth to Campbeltown run that she opened her career.

Between 1915 and 1919, with many of her consorts, **Queen Alexandra** was requisitioned as a military transport, and it was while employed in this work that she engaged, rammed, and sank a German U-Boat.

With the war behind her, **Queen Alexandra** was reconditioned and returned to her owners' service principally on the Princes Pier to Inveraray run. In 1927, however, she returned to the Campbeltown run.

In 1932, her upper deck below the shade deck was enclosed to form an observation lounge, and although her appearance was not enhanced by this alteration she was merely following the pattern which had been set by **King George V** in 1926.

In 1935 Turbine Steamers and its associate Company, Williamson Buchanan Steamers, were acquired by the L.M.S. Railway and David MacBrayne. Allocated to MacBrayne were **King George V** and **Queen Alexandra**. Although the white section of her funnels was immediately painted in MacBrayne's red, **Queen Alexandra,** as such, never sailed for her new owners. Emerging from James Lamont & Co's Yard in May 1936, the newly named, **Saint Columba**

was unrecognisable as the old **Queen Alexandra**. Her shade deck had been extended aft and given solid bulwarks at the forward end, a main mast had been fitted and three new slightly elliptical funnels had replaced the original two — the third being a dummy. **Saint Columba** was certainly impressive and was immediately placed on MacBrayne's prestigious 7.ll am run from Bridge Wharf to Govan, Princes Pier, Gourock, Dunoon, Innellan, Rothesay, Colintraive, Tighnabruaich, Tarbert and Ardrishaig - the first leg of the "Royal Route". The following year **Saint Columba** became the first Clyde steamer to be permanently converted to burn oil fuel.

During the Second World War the Clyde's turbines virtually escaped requisition, although **Saint Columba** was used as an accommodation vessel at Greenock.

After the war, **Saint Columba** returned to a truncated Royal Route from Gourock instead of from Glasgow. In 1947, on account of the poor state of Colintraive Pier, berthing at the pier was no longer possible so a ferry boat came out from the pier to meet **Saint Columba**. Therafter the Colintraive call was omitted altogether. **Saint Columba's** post war years were remarkably incident free. She was never taken off the Firth of Clyde by MacBraynes and her only real mishap was to run aground in Ettrick Bay, Bute, in thick fog in 1953, before she was fitted with radar.

Old age and diminishing passenger numbers, however, took their toll, and after the 1958 season **Saint Columba** handed over the route to the smaller and more economical **Lochfyne.**

I.M.

Tr.S.S. Duchess of Montrose

Denny of Dumbarton launched a very notable vessel for the Clyde passenger fleet in 1930. She was given the title **Duchess of Montrose** and was the second steamer in the Caledonian Steam Packet Company to carry this name.

The former "Duchess" was a neat little paddleboat, built 28 years previously, and the new vessel, while greatly exceeding her forebear in tonnage, was likewise a distinguished looking craft.

Before the advent of the turbine **King George V** in 1926, all the members of the Clyde pleasure flotilla had their promenade decks open to the elements. The Williamson boat, however, had part of this deck enclosed to form an observation lounge and **Duchess of Montrose** was also constructed on this pattern. Large windows made it a popular focal point with the passengers. As a result of this and other amenities, such as a cosy lounge below and a dining saloon on the main deck, the vessel was rated as a one class ship. No steerage fares were issued.

On trial, her turbine machinery drove her at over 20 knots and altogether she was a worthwhile addition to the estuary.

If there was one blemish to mar her outline, it was the short pole mast aft, but this was heightened to full mainmast standard in 1934, though her looks might have been further enhanced had the builders been content with a foremast only.

Her home berth was at Gourock and her summer cruising took her to Ayr, round Arran and Ailsa Craig or on the ever popular "round the lochs" excursion. For a few years she even essayed the longer journey down to Stranraer.

During the years of war she was not called up to serve with the Royal Navy as were many of her sisters, but it was then that she probably experienced the most strenuous period of her career. Repainted, sometime in dark ochre upperworks and black hull, sometime all-over grey, she was based at Wemyss Bay, below the Cloch-Dunoon anti-submarine boom. From there she plied an almost continual four seasons ferry service to Rothesay, her afterdeck often piled high with goods.

With the return of peace, **Duchess of Montrose** pursued a modified version of her pre-war cruising, with frequent voyages to Arran and Inveraray.

In May, 1945, **King George V** (now a unit of the MacBrayne fleet) suffered a machinery defect and for a time the "Duchess" deputised for her on the Tarbert and Ardrishaig route.

The following year, the Clyde experienced something of an Indian summer and in early October there was a one-day freak fog. Around Rothesay Bay and up river off Ashton the atmosphere was crystal clear, but all along the Cowal shore the mist bank lurked dense and menacing.

On this particular day **Duchess of Montrose** vanished into the murk on her afternoon run to Kirn, etc., but she failed to make the pier. Instead she embedded her bow on the rocky Cowal shore, so gently that few of her passengers were aware of her plight, but with sufficient force as to defy the combined efforts of her colleagues, **King Edward, Duchess of Hamilton** and **Marchioness of Lorne**, to drag her clear. Tugs had to be called in to free her.

Under state control the "Duchess" deviated little in her post-war cruising, although latterly she was a frequent visitor to Campbeltown.

In 1965, with the cut in the Clyde services, **Duchess of Montrose** was laid up in Albert Harbour, Greenock, her finery dulling to drabness in the months of enforced idleness. As no reprieve was forthcoming, she was taken in tow to Ghent and to oblivion in the scrap yard.

G.S.

T. S. "QUEEN MARY II"   J. NICHOLSON

Tr.S.S. Queen Mary

The departure of the paddle steamer **Isle of Arran** in the spring of 1933 did not for long leave a gap in the ranks of the Clyde up river fleet, for a ship of much greater tonnage was just about ready to replace the **Isle of Arran**, which went for service on the Thames.

The new ship was fitted out in Denny's yard and had been named **Queen Mary** on March 30. She was the last Clyde pleasure boat to bear a regal title, once so popular. She was also the first turbine vessel to be constructed for the Bridge Wharf run and, if perhaps of not so fine a line as some of the Denny ships, was an extremely comfortable craft in which to travel.

Queen Mary introduced some novel features in design on the Firth. Her cabin passengers were housed in the forepart of the ship and her boat deck extended right aft, almost to the stern, thus affording the steerage class not only a share of the top deck but also plenty of shelter without having to resort to the saloon below. Unlike the usual design of Clyde turbines she had a solid bulwark forward instead of an open rail and the passageway to her foredeck was via a stairway from the promenade deck instead of by the conventional doorway from the covered deck enclosures. The first class dining-saloon was also placed in the forepart of the vessel, while the second class contained a tearoom, sodabar, smokeroom and bar.

With a well raked mast just forward of the bridge, two heavily built funnels, a slightly raked stem and cruiser stern, the **Queen Mary** was an acquisition to the river fleet.

Under the command of Captain Donald McKinnon, she took up the 10 o'clock run to Dunoon and Rothesay with a cruise to Largs and the coast of Arran as Williamson-Buchanan's biggest carrier. She became so popular with Glasgow day trippers that it was not uncommon to find her turning away passengers.

After two seasons there came a change, not in the affection of the travelling public, but in her title. The new Cunard liner, so long known simply as "534" at John Brown's of Clydebank, was at last ready for launching and her owners were most anxious to bestow on her the name **Queen Mary**, for Her Majesty was to perform the naming ceremony. As a gesture of goodwill the proprietors of the Clyde turbine made this possible by changing the name of their ship to **Queen Mary II**.

The addition of the Roman numeral to her name was the only change in her appearance and she continued to serve right up to the outbreak of war (her wonderful carrying capacity often being fully taxed in midsummer). By then she had come under L.M.S. control.

During the war years, with the Cloch-Dunoon boom in operation her activities were confined to the upper reaches of the Firth. She divided her time between service runs to the Cowal shore and the transportation of troops to and from the many liners which arrived in the Clyde with servicemen from overseas.

With Captain Fergus Murdoch now in command she reopened the postwar all-the-way sailings on June 1, 1946, and continued on this service after nationalisation.

During the war years she had appeared in various disguises of paintwork; battleship grey, black hull and upperworks in ochre, and towards the close of hostilities all-over light grey (almost silver in its pallor). The 1950's saw sweeping changes. A mainmast was added in 1953 and, four years later, while being reboilered and converted to oil burning, her twin funnels were removed and a large, modern-looking oval one substituted. In 1969 her masts were shortened to enable her to pass under the Kingston Bridge, this being much to the detriment of her appearance.

The Bridge Wharf traffic declined to such an extent that all-the-way sailings were withdrawn after 1969 and **Queen Mary II** was based at Gourock in 1970. The following year, after a much needed refit, she succeeded **Duchess of Hamilton** on the Campbeltown and Inveraray runs.

In 1976 her name was changed back to **Queen Mary** but it was to be only for two seasons, as she was in turn replaced by **Glen Sannox**. After languishing in dock she eventually re-appeared in 1988 on the Thames as a replacement restaurant for **Old Caledonia**.

G.S.&I.M.

The publishers of this book have received a great deal of interest in their first title "Memories of the Clyde – The Duchess of Fife 1903–1953". Letters from as far apart as Thurso, Caithness in the north and Sidmouth, Devon in the south as well as Canada, the USA and Australia have been extremely complimentary about the quality of its production.

Some readers used the main deck and rigging plans to produce their own scale models and we take pleasure in reproducing here the scale model made by one reader T. McGrath of Leicestershire and photographed by his son M.D.C. McGrath.

The publishers welcome readers' letters re-counting their own "Memories of the Clyde" but regret that they may not be able to respond to every letter.